RAINFORESTS

CONTENTS

This edition is published by Southwater

Southwater is an imprint of
Anness Publishing Limited
Hermes House
88–89 Blackfriars Road
London SE1 8HA
tel. 020 7401 2077
fax 020 7633 9499

Distributed in the UK by
The Manning Partnership
251–253 London Road East
Batheaston
Bath BA1 7RL
tel. 01225 852 727
fax 01225 852 852

Distributed in the USA by
National Books Network
4720 Boston Way
Lanhan
MD 20706
tel. 301 459 3366
fax 301 459 1705

Distributed in Australia by
Sandstone Publishing
Unit 1, 360 Norton Street
Leichhardt
New South Wales 2040
tel. 02 9560 7888
fax 02 9560 7488

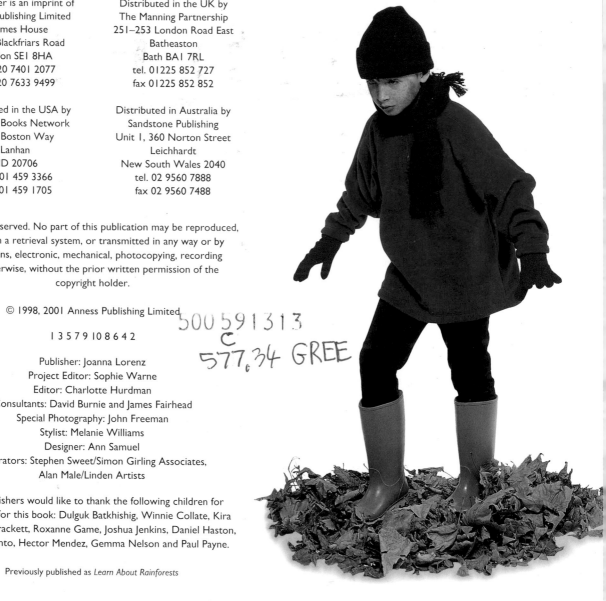

1 3 5 7 9 10 8 6 4 2

Publisher: Joanna Lorenz
Project Editor: Sophie Warne
Editor: Charlotte Hurdman
Consultants: David Burnie and James Fairhead
Special Photography: John Freeman
Stylist: Melanie Williams
Designer: Ann Samuel
Illustrators: Stephen Sweet/Simon Girling Associates,
Alan Male/Linden Artists

The publishers would like to thank the following children for
modelling for this book: Dulguk Batkhishig, Winnie Collate, Kira
Dunleavy Brackett, Roxanne Game, Joshua Jenkins, Daniel Haston,
Kieron Minto, Hector Mendez, Gemma Nelson and Paul Payne.

Previously published as *Learn About Rainforests*

Forest storeys

Rainforests are made up of four different storeys, or layers. The canopy is the dense, leafy layer at the top. The tallest trees, which rise above the forest canopy, are called emergents. The understorey is the layer between the canopy and the ground. The lowest layer is the forest floor.

Emergent trees poke above the canopy

The forest canopy forms a dense roof

Understorey plants thrive in shady places

Fewer plants grow on the forest floor

RAINFORESTS OF THE WORLD

THERE are several different types of rainforest. Tropical rainforests are found near the Equator, where it is warm and wet all the year round. There is little difference between the seasons. During the day, temperatures remain steady at about 30°C, and rain falls almost every afternoon. Trees and plants thrive in these even temperatures. Outside the tropics, cooler temperate rainforests are found. Here, temperatures are more varied and conditions are less regular. Most tropical forests are found in lowland areas. Lowland forest becomes montane, or cloud, forest on upland slopes, and mangrove forest at the coast and along rivers. Flooded forest is found alongside rivers, which burst their banks for several weeks each year. The division between different types of rainforest can be marked, but sometimes the types merge into one another with no clear division.

Flowers of the forest
Bright flowers bloom among the dense foliage of a tropical rainforest. Plants and trees thrive in the warm, moist conditions that are found all year round in tropical lowland forests.

Cloud forest
Montane forests are found on hills and mountains. Conditions are cooler and damper than in lowland forests. The upper slopes of these forests are permanently hidden in mist and fog, so they are also known as cloud forests.

Lowland rainforest
Most tropical rainforests are found in lowland areas. Plants and animals are most abundant in the canopy and understorey. Less wildlife lives on the forest floor than in cooler woods.

Flooded forest

Strips of land along the banks of slow-flowing rivers are covered in flooded forests. The rivers regularly burst their banks and flood the forest floor. Some flooded forests are permanently underwater. Even so, many kinds of trees and plants flourish here. The fertile soil is enriched with silt carried downstream by the river when it floods.

Temperate forest

Moss and ferns flourish on maple trees in the temperate rainforest along the west coast of North America. Daily temperatures vary more in temperate rainforests than in tropical jungles, but there is still plenty of rain. Temperate forests contain some of the world's tallest and oldest trees.

Mangrove forest

These swampy forests are found along tropical coastlines and river estuaries, where the soil is rich in silt and mud. Twice a day, the tides flood in and out. Mangroves have their roots in salty water, which is low in oxygen. They put out special roots above the surface to breathe.

THE TOPMOST TREES

RAINFOREST trees grow very tall, up to heights of 40 or 50 m. High above the ground, their leaves spread out to form the forest canopy. Stretching up, above the canopy, are emergents which reach up to 70 m in height - the tallest trees in the rainforest. The upper canopy is also home to smaller plants, such as orchids and bromeliads. These plants grow and flower high above the ground, but they are not rooted in forest soil. Instead, they root on to the branches of forest trees. Plants that grow on other plants without harming them are known as epiphytes or air plants. Many of the plants have leaves with a smooth, waxy surface to prevent them from losing too much water. Colourful birds and agile monkeys make their home amongst these plants. These animals are small and light, as the slender twigs and stems here would not support the weight of heavier animals.

Skilful climbers
Small monkeys, such as this capuchin, are very agile. They leap and scramble among the branches. Their tails help with balance, and some monkeys can even wind their tails round branches.

Emergent layer
Tall emergent trees rise above the Amazon rainforest canopy in Brazil. Emergents have long, straight trunks and leafy crowns that spread out like umbrellas. The tallest of all emergents, the tualang tree, can be found growing in South East Asia. It can grow up to 70 m above the ground.

Conures

These noisy, brightly coloured birds live in the upper canopy. They flutter from tree to tree, gorging themselves on fruit, seeds, flowers and insects. Conures are a species of parrot. The hooked beak is used to tear at fruit and open seeds. Conures also use their beaks to help them climb.

Walking in the air

Scientists knew little about the plants and animals of the upper canopy until recently, because it was very difficult to reach the species there to study them. Now, scientists string walkways between high tree trunks or build tall observation towers.

Air plant

This pink orchid growing on a rainforest tree in Brazil is an epiphytic air plant, which means it grows on the tree but is not a parasite. The orchid does not take nourishment or water from the host tree. Instead, it simply uses it as a stepping stone to reach the light.

Drip-tips

In the upper canopy, the leaves of many plants have a special shape, which tapers to a point called a drip-tip. This shape allows excess water to run off the plant after heavy rain, helping to prevent harmful algae growing on the leaves.

FOREST SURVEY

Kauri pines
Kauris grow in temperate
rainforest in New Zealand.
Like many trees, their trunks
are distinctive, growing tall
and straight to reach the light.

A small area of rainforest holds many different species, or kinds, of trees. In some rainforests, you can walk for more than an hour without coming across the same species twice. One of the first jobs for scientists working in a rainforest is to identify all the trees in their study area. Both in the rainforest and in your local area, trees can be identified by looking at their general size and shape. You can also study their bark, leaves and flowers, and look for clues such as fruits and nuts.

In tropical rainforests, most trees stay green all year round. In countries with a temperate (moderate) climate, many trees shed their leaves in autumn. The shape of the trunk and branches can also help to identify a tree. When studying trees, scientists record their girth (the distance around the trunk), measuring at chest height. You can survey and identify the trees in a local park or wood using the same methods. Choose an area of mixed woodland with many different sorts of trees. Always remember to take an adult with you to keep you safe.

MATERIALS

*You will need: field guide to local trees,
notebook, pen, coloured pencils.*

Identifying trees

1 Walk along a path in your chosen area. Try to identify the trees you find there from their general height and shape, using a field guide.

2 Bark can help you identify some trees. Silver birch bark is smooth and white with dark cracks. Match the bark with pictures in your guide.

3 Study leaf shapes, fruits and seeds. Identify trees with the help of a field guide, and record them in your notebook.

Seeds from a lime tree

Leaf from a plane tree

Acorn and its cup from an oak tree

A conker and its case from a horse chestnut tree

Seeds from a sycamore tree

Hips and leaves from a cockspur thorn

MATERIALS

You will need: sticky tape, string, gloves, metre ruler or tape measure, pen, notebook, coloured pencils, field guide, graph paper.

Make a chart with drawings of the trees you found and record their girths.

1 square = 5 cm

Cyprus

Beech

Horse chestnut

Cherry

Silver birch

Measuring a tree's girth

1 Stick a piece of tape on a piece of string. Wrap the string around a trunk at chest height. Mark where it meets the tape with your finger.

2 Lay the string along the ruler to find the length. Measure another tree of the same species. Is its girth the same? Why might they differ?

3 Make a chart with drawings of the trees you found. The trees with the thickest trunks are usually older than those with slender trunks.

RAINFOREST CANOPY

Plants of the understorey
Understorey plants include shrubs and smaller trees such as palms. Epiphytes and climbers festoon the branches.

THE trees of the forest canopy form a dense, leafy layer, 40 to 50 m above the ground and 10 to 15 m thick. The trees of the forest canopy spread their branches to catch most of the rain and sunlight. Below the canopy, the understorey is drier and more shady. Epiphytes, such as ferns and bromeliads, grow here as well as in the upper canopy. Vines and climbing lianas twist up from the forest floor towards the light. The canopy and understorey are home to a great variety of animals. Bats, birds and flying insects flit among the branches, gathering food. Most animals that cannot fly are good climbers. Some, such as flying squirrels and flying lizards, can glide between the trees. Other animals only visit the canopy on their way up to the treetops from the ground. Other creatures spend their whole lives in the branches, rarely dropping down to the forest floor.

Tamandua
This mammal's favourite food is termites. It uses its long snout and sticky tongue to probe inside termites' nests to lick out the insects. Sharp claws and a long tail help it to clamber among the branches of the rainforest canopy.

Macaws
Macaws are brightly coloured parrots. They use their powerful, hooked beaks to crack open nuts and seeds. Their short wings help them to fly and manoeuvre through the crowded canopy.

Bromeliads

The branches of this rainforest tree in Brazil are covered in bromeliads. High in the air, without roots in the soil, bromeliads must conserve, or save, as much moisture as they can. Some bromeliads collect rainwater in cups formed from rings of their waxy leaves. Insects and tiny frogs live in these small pools, even breeding there.

Climbing liana

Lianas are climbing plants with long, slender stems. They use the trunks of trees for support as they spiral upwards towards the light. At the top, they put out leaves, shoots and colourful flowers. Some lianas send down special roots called aerial roots to gather nourishing minerals from the soil. These roots may thicken to become gnarled, woody stems.

Strangler fig

This climbing plant eventually kills the host tree that supports it. A young fig lives high in the branches. As it grows, it sends down roots to the forest floor. The roots spread and then put out branches, which twine around the host tree and enclose it. Eventually the host dies, rotting away to leave a hollow network of fig stems.

PLANTS OF THE CANOPY

PLANTS cannot move around to find their food as animals do. Instead, they make their own. The leaves and stems of plants are green because they contain a substance called chlorophyll. The green cells work like tiny solar panels, using the energy from sunlight to combine carbon dioxide gas from the air and water from the ground to produce the plant's sugary food and oxygen. This amazing process is called photosynthesis.

In a rainforest, plants of the canopy and understorey are in competition for the light. When a tree or branch falls, plants and seedlings grow quickly, each rushing to spread its leaves in the extra light. The same search for light can be seen in the experiment below with cress seedlings. To get closer to the light, epiphytes such as bromeliads perch on high branches in the rainforest. Find out more about epiphytes (air plants) by growing them at home.

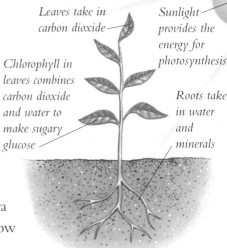

Leaves take in carbon dioxide

Sunlight provides the energy for photosynthesis

Chlorophyll in leaves combines carbon dioxide and water to make sugary glucose

Roots take in water and minerals

Through photosynthesis, plants use the energy in sunlight to make their food.

You will need: water, kitchen paper, two small plastic seed trays, cress seeds, watering can.

Reaching for the light

1 Place a layer of damp kitchen paper on the bottom of two seed trays. Sprinkle cress seeds sparingly over the top of the paper.

2 Water the seeds regularly. Store both trays in a dark place for a few days until the cress has sprouted. Then move one to a sunny place and leave the other in the dark.

Grown in a sunny place, seedlings are thick and healthy.

Left in the dark, seedlings grow tall and spindly to reach the light.

Grow your own air plant

1 Wearing gloves, wrap moss around one end of the branch or driftwood. Tie the moss securely in place with cotton thread.

2 Pile gravel into a sturdy plant pot until the pot is almost full. You could use a trowel to help you transfer the gravel.

3 Now push the wood down into the gravel, until it stands up in the pot without tipping it over. Spray the moss with water.

MATERIALS

You will need: gloves, sphagnum moss, branch or piece of driftwood, cotton thread, trowel, gravel, plant pot, water spray, air plants (from a garden centre), glue, liquid plant-food.

4 Arrange the air plants by pressing them gently into the moss. A drop of glue on the base of the plant will help hold it in place.

5 Spray the plants from time to time with water. A few drops of liquid plant-food will help the plants to grow.

Air plants grow well indoors and make an unusual display. They do not need soil to grow, but instead they wrap their roots around a branch.

THE FOREST FLOOR

THE forest floor is dim and shady. The dense leafy layer of the canopy above blocks out most of the light. The plants of the canopy absorb much of the water. After a heavy rain shower, it may take as long as ten minutes for water to drip down through the leaves to the ground. Where sunlight reaches the ground, along the banks of rivers and in forest clearings, the undergrowth is dense and lush. Elsewhere, the lack of light means that fewer plants and shrubs live down at ground level than in the canopy above. You might think that the soil in a tropical rainforest would be rich and fertile. In fact it is thin and poor, because the rainforest plants quickly take up all the goodness in the soil. Little grass grows in the forest. Instead, the ground is covered by leaf litter – a thick carpet of fallen leaves. The leaves rot quickly, broken down by insects and other minibeasts to enrich the soil. In the dappled light, larger animals such as tapir, small deer and rodents sift through the leaves in search of food.

Plants of the forest floor
Ferns and flowering plants thrive in pools of sunlight created by a fallen tree. Elsewhere it is too shady for most plants to flourish. However, fungi and parasitic plants (those that feed off other plants) thrive in dim light.

The scarlet flowers of this heliconia make a bright splash of colour in a forest clearing in Cuba. When a mighty forest tree falls, other plants are quick to take advantage of the increased light.

Buttress roots
In most rainforests, only a thin layer of soil covers the ground. To anchor themselves firmly, large trees grow special roots called buttress roots. Thin wings of very hard wood rise from roots in the ground and act as buttresses to support the tree's weight.

Python

The orange and black markings on this python help to hide it among fallen leaves on the forest floor. Camouflage is an important weapon as it lies in wait for prey. Pythons are constrictors, which means they kill their prey by wrapping themselves around their victims and squeezing them to death.

Parasitic plant

The *Balanophora elongata* is a parasitic plant that grows on the roots of rainforest trees in Southeast Asia. It attaches itself to the host plant's roots where it steals food and water, diverting the nutrients for itself. Because it does not make its own food, it does not need green leaves or sunlight.

Tapir

The tapir uses its long, flexible, upper lip to tear leaves and shoots from plants as it browses in the undergrowth. These shy, pig-like animals are active mainly at night.

17

STUDYING THE FOREST FLOOR

TROPICAL rainforests are amazingly rich in plant and animal life. As many as 50 plant species can grow on just one tree, and new species of plants are identified every week. Biologists working in rainforests use a square frame called a quadrat to help them record all the plants living in a patch of forest soil. You can use the same method to survey the plant life in your local wood. Beneath the ground, the forest teems with life. Minibeasts such as worms, slugs, millipedes and beetles make their way through the soil. Much smaller creatures, such as mites, which can only be seen with a microscope, also live here. All these creatures feed on dead plant and animal matter. Bacteria and fungi break down everything that remains, helping to create a rich fertilizer for the plants. As leaves rot down, they return their goodness to the soil. Leaves and other plant material decay quickest in warm, moist areas.

Studying plant life
Botanists (scientists who study plants) take samples and measure the depth of the leaf layer in the Amazon rainforest. Creatures feeding on the forest floor help to release the nutrients contained in dead leaves and fallen branches.

MATERIALS

You will need: gloves, eight pegs, metre ruler or tape measure, string, field guide, pen, notebook, coloured pencils, graph paper.

Carrying out a plant survey

1 Choose a patch of ground to sample and put in a peg. Measure 1 m with the ruler and put in another peg. Stretch string between the pegs.

2 Now measure the remaining sides, pushing in two more pegs and stretching string between them to mark out one square metre.

Plant survey chart

3 Measure and mark the midpoint of each side with pegs. Stretch string between these pegs to divide the square into quarters.

4 Use your field guide to help you identify the plant species growing in each quarter of the square. Do different plants grow in each area?

5 Draw a chart on graph paper to record the position of each plant. Use different colours for each plant type you found. Add up the totals.

MATERIALS

You will need: gloves, two clean plastic containers, one lid, soil, dead leaves, water in a watering can.

After a few weeks, the leaves in the wet soil (left) will have begun to rot, while those in the dry soil (right) will have shrivelled.

Watching decay in the soil

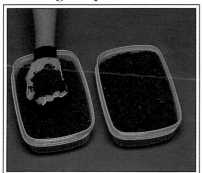

1 Be sure to wear gloves for this project. Use your hand or a trowel to fill two plastic containers with plenty of dry soil.

2 Put leaves on top of the soil in one container. Water the leaves and soil throughly, then cover up the container by pressing on the lid.

3 Put dry leaves on top of the soil in the other container, but do not cover it. Store both containers in a dry place such as a garden shed.

LIFE-GIVING JUNGLES

RAINFORESTS cover only a tiny fraction of the Earth's surface, yet they affect the air we breathe and influence weather patterns around the world. During photosynthesis, plants and trees take in carbon dioxide from the air and give out oxygen. Humans and all other animals need oxygen to breathe. Rainforests help to maintain the right balance of gases in our atmosphere. They also act like giant sponges. When it rains, they soak up water that would otherwise run straight into rivers and out to sea. The trees suck up the moisture through their roots and later release it into the air again in the form of a gas called water vapour. High in the air, the tiny drops of water gather together to form clouds, which bring rain. By helping to cause rain, forests bring life to drier areas. If rainforests are cut down, clouds will not gather and less rain will fall. Drought and crop failure may follow in areas hundreds of kilometres away.

Torrential rain
Heavy rain is common in tropical rainforests. The roots of trees and plants absorb much of the water. The rest trickles away to feed streams and rivers.

The water cycle
Water circulates through the Earth's atmosphere in a continuous cycle. The rainforests are an important part of this cycle. Heat from the Sun causes moisture to evaporate off leaves and from oceans (1). Water vapour in the air then forms rain clouds (2). When it rains, trees absorb some of the water through their roots. Much of this rain is carried back to the oceans via streams and rivers (3). Sunlight heats the oceans, causing water to evaporate into the air again (4).

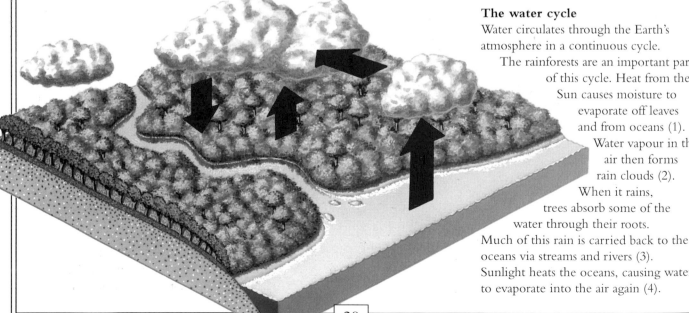

Oxygen given out

Carbon dioxide taken in

Mirror effect

The rainforest canopy is like a dark green blanket. Dark colours absorb sunlight and heat better than light colours. Where parts of the forest are cut down, light-coloured vegetation grows up. This reflects back more light, warming up the atmosphere.

During photosynthesis trees and plants take in carbon dioxide and give out oxygen.

Keeping the air fresh

Trees help to top up levels of oxygen in the Earth's atmosphere. This is the reverse of what humans and animals do. Their lungs breathe in oxygen and breathe out carbon dioxide.

The greenhouse effect

Burning vegetation releases carbon dioxide and other gases into the air. These gases trap the Sun's heat in the atmosphere, a bit like the glass in a greenhouse. This causes world temperatures to rise – an effect called global warming.

Melting ice

Glaciers like this one in Antarctica may well be affected by the burning of rainforests thousands of kilometres away. If global warming continues, glaciers and icecaps in the Arctic and Antarctic may start to melt. If this happens, sea-levels will rise around the world and low-lying coastal areas will be threatened by flooding.

RAINFOREST PLANTS

LIKE all living things, rainforest plants need water to live. They take up water through their roots. Water travels up through the plant's stem, and from there is taken to the leaves, shoots and flowers. Water carries the soil's nutrients to all parts of the plant. In the leaves, the nutrients and water are needed for photosynthesis. Excess water not needed by the plant evaporates back into the air in the form of a gas called water vapour. The water vapour escapes through tiny holes in the leaves called stomata. This process is called transpiration.

Find out more about transpiration by trying the experiment below. The experiment uses coloured water to show how water travels straight up a plant's stem, not across it. The water travels in tough-walled tubes called xylem. The flower used is a carnation, but the experiment will work just as well with a pale-coloured daisy or a chrysanthemum.

Sucking up water

Half-fill two jars with water and mark the level. Add a little oil (it will float on top). Put a twig in one jar. Check the levels next day. The water in the twig's jar will be lower. Water cannot evaporate through oil, so the twig has sucked it up.

MATERIALS

You will need: water, two tall glasses, water-soluble ink or food dye, a white carnation, scissors, sticky tape.

Transpiration in colour

1 Pour some water into two tall drinking glasses. Add drops of ink or food dye to one jar to give the water a strong, bright colour.

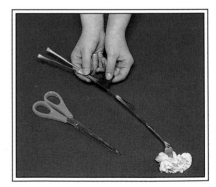

2 Split the stem of the carnation lengthwise to about half-way up the stem. Bind the stem with tape so it does not split any further.

3 Place the jars side by side, and stand one half of the stem in each jar. Lean the flower against a window if it will not stand up.

4 After a few hours, check what has happened. One half of the flower will be coloured with the dye, the other will remain white.

Coloured water is drawn up one side of the stem. It has turned the petals on that side pink.

You will need: house plant, watering can, clear plastic bag, sticky tape, scissors.

Evaporation in action

Moisture, given off by the plant as water vapour, condenses, or turns back to water, when it touches the sides of the plastic bag.

1 Water the house plant well using a watering can. It is best to water the plant from the base, or water just the soil.

2 Place the plastic bag over the plant, taking care not to damage the leaves. Tape the bag tightly around the pot. Leave overnight.

3 Inside the bag, water vapour given off by the plant turns back into water. The air inside is warm and moist, like the air in a rainforest.

RAINFOREST CYCLES

LIKE most plants and trees, those that grow in the rainforest reproduce by making seeds, which sprout and grow into new plants. To produce seeds, plants must be fertilized by pollen, usually from another plant of the same species. Most rainforest plants are pollinated by animals – mainly insects, such as bees and butterflies, but also birds and even bats. These animals are attracted to the sugary nectar which plants produce and to the bright colours and strong scents of their flowers. When an animal reaches into a flower to feed on nectar, pollen rubs off on its body. The pollen is transferred to the next plant the creature visits and fertilizes it. After fertilization, the plant makes seeds, which must be spread as far away as possible. The seeds of some jungle plants are spread by water and a few are carried on the wind, but most rely on animals to spread their seeds. Seeds often develop inside juicy fruits. When an animal eats the fruit, it spits out the seeds or passes them in its droppings away from the parent plant.

Insect partners
Some plants are pollinated by many different kinds of insects. Orchids, however, are often pollinated by a single species – often bees. To attract bees, orchids use bright colours and special scents, some are even shaped like bees.

Bird helpers
A tiny hummingbird reaches inside a flower with the help of its long beak and tongue. As it does so, its beak and body are dusted with pollen grains. Plants pollinated by birds often produce brightly coloured flowers, because birds see bright colours clearly.

FACT BOX

• To hover in front of flowers to feed, hummingbirds beat their wings up to 80 times a second – faster than the human eye can see. The sound of their fluttering wings gives the birds their name.

• The sausage tree of Madagascar is pollinated by bats. The tree is named after the shape of its fruits.

• Sago palm trees produce fruits inside scaly cases with a corky layer, so that the fruit can float on water.

Night pollinators

Some plants are pollinated by fruit bats (*above*) or moths, creatures that are active at dusk or when it is dark. The flowers open at night and have strong scents to attract the animals. Brightly coloured flowers are less effective at night, because their colours do not show up in the dark.

Blowing in the wind

The kapok is one of the few rainforest trees whose seeds are spread by the wind. These tall trees rise above the canopy, where there are more air currents. When the kapok pod splits open, the tuft of threads inside carry the tiny seeds away on the wind.

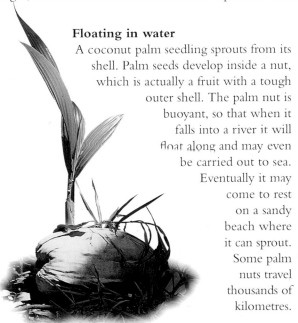

Floating in water

A coconut palm seedling sprouts from its shell. Palm seeds develop inside a nut, which is actually a fruit with a tough outer shell. The palm nut is buoyant, so that when it falls into a river it will float along and may even be carried out to sea. Eventually it may come to rest on a sandy beach where it can sprout. Some palm nuts travel thousands of kilometres.

Travelling seeds

Pacas are rodents from South and Central America. They forage for roots, seeds, fruits and berries at night on the forest floor. The seeds inside the fruit travel through the animal unharmed and pass out later in its droppings. The seeds, with their ready-made packet of fertilizer, root and quickly start to grow.

LOOKING AT PLANT CYCLES

You will need: gloves, field guide, collecting pot, muslin, rubber band, notebook, coloured pencils.

THE plants in your local area disperse, or spread, their seeds in the same ways that rainforest plants do. If you take a close look at seeds, you will be able to tell how they are spread. All over the world, you can find plants that produce seeds inside plump, juicy fruits. When birds and mammals eat the fruits, they spread the seeds. Other plants produce fruits with tiny hooks that catch in animal fur. They may be carried for some distance before they drop off on to the ground and take root. Temperate areas are often windier than rainforests, so more plants produce light seeds that drift in the air.

Once seeds are spread, they germinate (root and grow) if the light, warmth and moisture conditions are right. On the shady rainforest floor, seeds may wait for years before a tree crashes down, leaving a space that provides enough light for the seeds to grow. Indoors, in warm conditions, it can be easy to get rainforest seeds to grow. Try germinating an avocado plant from its stone, but make sure the atmosphere is warm and humid enough.

Looking at seed dispersal

1 In woods and parks, look out for nibbled nuts and acorns. These seeds are nutritious food for many animals. Squirrels bury stores of seeds, which may germinate later.

2 Visit your local pond or stream to find seeds that are dispersed by water, such as alders. Use your field guide to identify any seeds you see floating on the water.

3 Maple and sycamore trees have light seeds with wings. As they fall, the wings spin the seed through the air, helping it to fly farther and germinate far from the parent tree.

4 Plants such as dandelions have very light seeds, each with its own small parachute of fine threads. These are carried away by the wind.

5 The seed capsules of poppies are like pepper pots with hundreds of tiny seeds inside. As the wind shakes the capsule, the seeds spill out.

6 When you walk through long grass, you may find burrs — fruits with tiny hooks — stuck on to your coat or to a pet's fur. Burrs may be carried a long way before they rub off.

MATERIALS

You will need: avocado stone, three cocktail sticks, jar filled with water, gloves, pot, trowel, potting compost.

Growing plants from tropical seeds

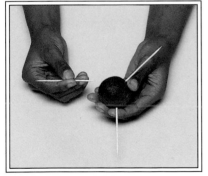

1 An avocado stone is the seed of the avocado plant. Clean off any flesh left on the stone and then carefully push three cocktail sticks into the stone, as shown above.

2 Fill a jar with water and suspend the stone so that it just touches the water line. Keep the jar in a warm, shady place and top up the water regularly.

3 When roots begin to grow down, plant the stone in a pot filled with compost. Place the pot where the air is warm and humid and wait for your seedling to grow.

THE THREATENED FOREST

ALL around the world, rainforests are being cut down at an alarming rate. At the beginning of the 20th century, they covered about twice the area they do today. Recently, the pace of destruction has increased. Experts estimate that an area of rainforest about the size of England is lost each year. There are many reasons for this. One of the main causes is logging – the felling of trees for timber. Many rainforest trees are made of valuable hardwoods, such as teak and mahogany, which are used for building houses and making furniture. But hardwood trees grow slowly and cannot be replaced quickly. Trees are also cleared to create new pasture for cattle. The poor quality of the forest soil means farming quickly exhausts it, so more trees must be cleared. Roads are cut through the forest and large areas are disturbed.

Carted away
Giant logs are loaded on to a truck in Papua New Guinea to be carried to the nearest port or paper mill. Rich businessmen make large profits from the timber trade while local people receive very little.

Cut down for fuel
Many developing countries depend on rainforests for fuel and firewood. Here, a kiln is being built to turn trees into charcoal, a better and more efficient fuel than wood alone.

Cabbage crop
This field in Malaysia has been cleared from forest land for growing cabbages. Forest soil is too poor to grow crops for long. In just a few years' time, the soil will be exhausted.

Terraced rice fields

Hilly forest land in Indonesia has been cleared and built up into terraces to grow rice. All over Southeast Asia, rainforest has been cut down to make these rice paddies. Terraces have been built for centuries, but now the region's growing population puts greater pressure on forest land.

Cattle ranching

Land that is not fertile enough for crops is often sold to cattle ranchers to graze their animals. But in a few years, even the grass is of such poor quality that the cattle must be moved on to fresh pastures. Land that once sustained a rainforest and all its animals and plants becomes useless.

Mining

A gold mine in Brazil scars forest land. Mining is another major cause of forest destruction. International corporations dig for oil, coal and valuable ores (metal-bearing rock) as well as precious metals such as gold and silver. As with the logging industry, large companies make big profits at the expense of the land and local people.

THE SELF-SUFFICIENT FOREST

MATERIALS

You will need: potted plant, plant pot filled with compost or soil, two plastic cups, two watering cans.

WHEN rainforest trees are cut down, even the soil is threatened. The roots of trees and plants help to hold the thin forest soil together. When the trees are felled, the soil is left bare. In heavy rainfall, the earth is washed away. This is called erosion. The project below will show you what happens. When rainforests are left alone, however, they sustain themselves indefinitely, recycling water and goodness from the soil. See how recycling works by growing a mini-jungle in a large bottle. The bottle reproduces the warm, moist conditions found in the rainforest. Inside the bottle, the plants are kept at an even temperature and are protected from draughts. They recycle their own moisture so they rarely need watering.

Destructive deforestation
Soil washes quickly off hillsides once covered with rainforest trees, like these in Madagascar. The soil builds up downstream to clog rivers and streams, which may then burst their banks and cause flooding.

Looking at soil erosion

1 Fit the potted plant into the neck of one of the plastic cups. Place the pot with only soil in it into the neck of the other cup.

2 Pour water on to the plant and into the pot of soil. What happens?

Water passes quickly through the pot without the plant. It is muddy because more soil is washed through.

Water passes more slowly through the plant. It will trickle through almost clear.

Plant a mini-jungle

1 Wash out your bottle to make sure it is clean. Place handfuls of gravel into the bottom of the bottle, to make the lowest layer.

2 Mix a little charcoal with the potting compost. Add a deep layer of compost mixture and then smooth out the level of the soil.

3 Make holes for the plants in the soil with a spoon or trowel. Then gently lower the plants into the holes you have made.

MATERIALS

You will need: large plastic bottle or jar with a lid, gloves, gravel, charcoal, potting compost, spoon or trowel, small tropical plants, plant sprayer or watering can with sprinkler rose.

Moisture from the plants will condense on the sides of the bottle. It will then drip down into the soil, to be reused.

6 Put the lid on the bottle, and your mini-jungle is complete! Water is recycled inside the bottle, so you will not need to water your jungle often.

4 Firm the soil down around the base of each plant. Use a spoon or trowel if you cannot reach that far with your fingers.

5 Mist the plants and soil quite thoroughly with water from a plant spray, or using a watering can with a sprinkler attachment.

THE WEB OF LIFE

RAINFORESTS support a wide variety of life, in a web that contains thousands of plant and animal species. In a tropical forest, plant food is available all year round. Herbivores (plant-eating animals) thrive on many different kinds of vegetation, including leaves, shoots, flowers, fruit and nuts. Carnivores (meat-eating animals) prey on, or hunt, the herbivores and weaker carnivores. Prey animals are constantly alert to the danger of being killed and eaten. To survive, carnivores must first find, then catch and kill their prey. Animals that kill and eat other animals are called predators. They have keen senses to help them in the hunt. Predators use different means of catching their prey. Big cats rely on strength and speed to outrun their victims. Other hunters, such as snakes, use stealth to pounce on an unsuspecting animal.

Blood-sucker
The vampire bat preys on large mammals such as cattle, but does not kill its victims. Instead, it uses its sharp front teeth to puncture the animal's skin. The bat's saliva prevents the animal's blood clotting as it laps it from the wound.

Winged carnivore
Harpy eagles are fierce predators that live high in the treetops. They prey on monkeys and small mammals scrambling about in the branches in search of fruit. The eagle swoops down and kills its prey with its sharp claws, or talons.

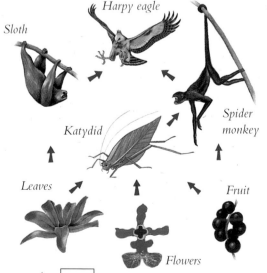

Harpy eagle

Sloth

Katydid

Spider monkey

Leaves

Fruit

Flowers

Food web
The links between life in a tropical forest can be shown by a food web. At the bottom are plants, which make their own food. Herbivores eat the plants and in turn they may be eaten by carnivores. Animals that eat both plants and animals are called omnivores. This diagram shows part of a food web in South America.

Plant-eater

In South American forests, sloths hang from the branches, feeding on leaves. Their plant food is easy to find, but it is not very nourishing so sloths need to save as much energy as possible. They do so by moving very slowly and spending most of their time resting.

Vipers swallow their prey whole, as they have no teeth for chewing.

Top predator

Jaguars prey on many different kinds of animals, including cattle, pigs, terrapins and dogs. Their spotted coats help them to keep well hidden as they track their prey. The jaguar is at the top of its food chain and has little to fear from other animals, except humans.

Stealthy hunter

Vipers prey on birds and small mammals. They lie in wait hidden by leaves on the forest floor. If a victim comes too close, the snake lunges forward with a deadly bite. Its fangs inject poison, which kills the animal very quickly.

ANIMAL TRACKS

THE animals of your local woodland search for their food in similar ways to the creatures of the rainforest. Wild creatures are very wary and will disappear into the forest at the slightest hint of danger. You can learn a lot about animals, however, by looking at their tracks. Look for

You will need: gloves, field guide, magnifying glass, notebook, pencil, camera.

footprints in soft mud or sand, or wherever the ground is wet. The banks of streams or rivers are often criss-crossed by animal prints. In winter, tracks are very easy to see after a snow fall. Tracks can give clues about the size and weight of the animal that made them. They also show how animals move – whether they run, hop, slide or slither. Compare the tracks you find to pictures in a field guide. Different groups of animals (mammals, birds, reptiles and amphibians) leave very different tracks. Draw the footprints or take a photograph and keep a record in your notebook. Try making a plaster cast of an animal print you find.

These are the footprints of a wild Asian elephant. They were made in the bottom of a dried-up river bed.

Looking at animal tracks

1 When you find a footprint, count the number of toes. Can you see any claws? A fox's paw is rounded, with four toes and claws.

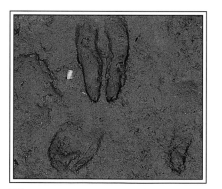

2 Deer have narrow, split hooves with two toes. They leave deep tracks because they walk with all their weight on their toes.

3 Most birds have long, spindly feet, with three or four toes. Some wading birds have webbed feet, which leave distinctive prints.

Making a footprint cast

1 Find a clear animal track either in sand or dry mud. Remove any loose twigs or leaves around the print, (remember to wear gloves if working in soil).

2 Bend a strip of card into a ring large enough to fit around the print and secure it with a paper clip. Place the ring over the print.

3 Mix the plaster of Paris with a little water in a bowl, according to the packet's instructions. Stir until the mixture is thick and even.

MATERIALS

You will need: card, paper clip, plaster of Paris, water, mixing bowl, spoon, trowel, scrubbing brush, paintbrush, paints, waterpot.

Finished cast of a dog print

4 Carefully spoon enough plaster of Paris on to the print to cover it. After 15 minutes the cast will be dry enough for you to pick it up.

5 Use a trowel to prise the cast loose. Peel off the paper ring. Clean up the cast by brushing off any loose soil or sand.

6 Allow to dry for 24 hours. After this you could paint or varnish the cast.

WHAT IS IN THE WATER?

WATER is everywhere in a tropical rainforest. It drips down from the canopy to form swampy puddles in the soil and feeds gushing streams and rivers. The world's second longest river is the Amazon in South America, which flows for over 6,500 km from the Andes mountains to the Atlantic Ocean. Many different kinds of animals live in and along the river. There are 5,000 species of fish, including the arapaima, the world's largest freshwater fish, and the deadly piranha. Water mammals, such as huge otters and capybaras thrive, and there are many reptiles, including crocodiles, anacondas and a lizard that walks on water. As the river widens near the sea, dolphins and seal-like manatees live in the murky water.

The Amazon basin
The igapo and varzea are large areas of forest that flood regularly. Their plants are used to being underwater for up to six months every year.

Capybaras
These are the world's largest rodents and look a bit like giant guinea pigs. Capybaras live in family groups, spending a lot of time in the water. They are excellent swimmers with partly webbed feet.

Piranhas
These fish have razor-sharp teeth. They live on a diet of seeds and fruit, but also eat meat and can be dangerous to humans. A shoal of these river-fish can tear the flesh from an animal in a few minutes.

Basilisk lizards

The rainforests of South America are home to a remarkable reptile – a lizard that can walk on water. The basilisk lizard has flattened toes webbed with an extra fringe of scales. Using its tail to help with balance, the basilisk can drop on to water and run across the surface on its back legs to escape from a predator.

Anacondas

These giant reptiles are one of the world's largest snakes. An anaconda can grow up to 6 m long and weigh up to 225 kg. They are strong swimmers and spend much of their lives in the water. When hunting, they swim close to the shore, searching for prey animals as large as deer. They kill their victims by strangulation or by drowning them in the water.

Caimans

A kind of alligator, the caiman is found on the banks of rainforest rivers. It has a broad mouth for eating a wide variety of prey. When hunting, the caiman slides through the water, with just its eyes and nostrils showing above the surface. When it spots an animal drinking on the river bank, it approaches quietly, then pounces to seize its victim's snout. It drags the animal underwater and holds it down until it drowns. Caiman will grab whatever prey it can find and swallow fish and frogs whole.

RAINFOREST MINIBEASTS

INSECTS are the most numerous species on Earth, making up more than three-quarters of all known creatures. Insects outnumber human beings by 200 million to one. They are found in incredible numbers in tropical rainforests, and many species have not yet been named. Many, such as butterflies and bees, live high up in the canopy. Ants march along the branches of the understorey, while beetles and other minibeasts, such as spiders and centipedes, burrow among the leaves on the forest floor. Like larger forest animals, minibeasts eat all sorts of foods. Many feed on plants, but some are predators, hunting other minibeasts and even birds, small mammals and reptiles. Beetles and worms crunch up decaying plants and animals in the forest soil. Insects and other minibeasts are a vital food source for many larger animals. To protect themselves, many are coloured and patterned to blend in with their forest background. This method of disguise is called camouflage.

Golden beetle
This golden beetle is found in the cloud forest of Costa Rica in Central America. It feeds on ferns. When frightened, it lifts its tough, golden wing cases and spreads the delicate wings hidden underneath, before flying away.

Leaf-cutter ants
These ants scale the branches of high forest trees to collect leaves. They use their sharp jaws to bite off sections of leaf. The ants then carry them back to their underground nest, often travelling over 100 m to do so. There the leaves are chewed into a pulp and used to grow a special fungus, which the ants feed on.

FACT BOX

• More than 2000 different species of butterflies are found in the rainforests of South America.

• Leeches are sucking worms that fasten themselves firmly on to the skin of much larger animals to drink their blood. Once the leech has pierced the victim's skin, it gives off a substance, which prevents the animal's blood from clotting.

Flower mantis

This large insect is a praying mantis. The colour, shape and pattern of its body exactly imitate a tropical orchid. It waits for its prey, hidden against the flower. When an unwary creature comes too close, the mantis grabs it with its front legs and eats it alive.

Morpho butterfly

A morpho butterfly suns itself by resting with its wings open on a leaf in the rainforest. The bright blue colour of its wings is produced by light reflecting off tiny scales on the surface of the wing.

Bird-eating spider

Large spiders prey on birds, frogs and reptiles, as well as insects. This Chilean bird-eating spider lurks in leaves, lunging forward to attack its prey. Some spiders bite their prey, injecting poison through hollow fangs. Others spin silk thread and wrap it round a victim to immobilize it.

Katydid

This grasshopper-like insect is a katydid from Costa Rica. The round markings on its wings are called eyespots. When threatened, the katydid raises its eyespots, hoping to convince the enemy that it is large and dangerous.

LOOKING AT MINIBEASTS

N ATURALISTS who study insects and other small creatures in tropical rainforests have found an amazing variety of species. There are so many species that many do not have a common name, only a scientific one. To identify all the species living in a particular area, scientists mark off a quadrat or square and search all the possible places where small creatures hide – under leaves, stones and logs and in tiny crevices in tree trunks. They look for signs of feeding, such as chewed leaves or tiny holes in wood. They may leave pitfall traps in the ground, or hang traps in the trees. You can find and study minibeasts in your local area using the same methods. Wear gloves when handling these small creatures as some of them may sting or bite. Better still, use a small paintbrush to handle creatures or transfer them from your trap. Use a field guide to help identify them. When you have finished studying your creatures, take them back to where you found them and release them gently. Do not keep them captive for more than a few hours.

Swallowtail butterflies are found in many parts of the world, this one is from South America. Butterflies feed on rotten fruit as well as nectar. Try putting an over-ripe apple outside. What kinds of insect land on it to feed?

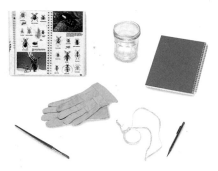

You will need:
gloves, paintbrush for picking up minibeasts, magnifying glass, field guide, collecting jar, notebook, pencil.

Finding minibeasts

1 Minibeasts such as worms and snails may shelter under rocks and stones. Gently replace the stones when you have finished your search.

2 Cracks in rotting wood may shelter woodlice and centipedes. Gently lift up rotting bark to find these creatures.

Make a pitfall trap

1 Ask an adult where you can dig a small hole in the garden. Use a trowel to dig a hole in damp earth, large enough for the jar to fit in.

2 Place the jar in the hole. Firm the earth back around the sides of the jar. Put small, fresh leaves in the bottom of the jar for bait.

3 Place small stones around the trap and balance a large flat stone or tile on top to prevent the trap filling up with rain. Leave overnight.

WARNING
Do not leave minibeasts in the trap for more than a few hours as they will die.

M A T E R I A L S
You will need: gloves, trowel, glass jar, small fresh leaves, small stones, large flat stone or tile, muslin cloth, elastic band, magnifying glass, field guide.

4 In the morning, remove the jar. Place a piece of muslin over the top and secure it with an elastic band. Study any minibeasts you have caught using a magnifying glass. Use a field guide to identify them.

5 When you have finished, release the creatures near where you found them.

This centipede has many pairs of legs, one pair on each body segment. A millipede is similar, but has two pairs of legs on each segment.

Adult insects, like this Queen wasp, have bodies in three main sections and six legs. Most have wings.

CENTRAL AMERICA

CENTRAL America forms a land bridge between the continents of North and South America. To the northeast lies the Caribbean Sea and the islands of Cuba, Hispaniola and Jamaica. This region was once entirely covered with rainforest, but large areas have been cleared for cattle ranching and for sugar cane plantations. Like other major rainforests, the jungles and mangrove swamps of Central America contain many plants and animals found nowhere else. The Caribbean islands are particularly rich in unique wildlife, because, in the past, there were few predators to hunt them there. Native plants of the region include many kinds of bromeliads and orchids, and cocoa trees whose pods are used to make chocolate.

Central America is famous for its large number of tropical birds, including many kinds of parrots. Some of these are now endangered, because they have been caught and sold in large numbers as pets. Monkeys, big cats, snakes and lizards slide or scramble through the trees in search of food.

Quetzal
The quetzal's spectacular feathers have a metallic sheen. The male has one of the longest tail plumes of any bird. This bird was once held sacred to the ancient Aztec and Mayan peoples, who worshipped it as the god of the air.

Howler monkey
The howler monkey is named after its loud, hooting call. Male monkeys call the loudest, to warn other monkeys away from the patch of the forest where their group is feeding. The monkey's large voice-box magnifies its call.

Green tree boa
A green tree boa lurks in the crook of a forest tree. Its green skin helps to camouflage it, allowing it to sneak up on animals such as deer and rodents. It coils its body around its prey and squeezes it to death before swallowing the victim whole.

Kinkajou

This member of the raccoon family has yellowish fur and a long tail. Its tail is prehensile, which means it can be used to hold on to branches. It uses its tail as a climbing aid as it clambers high in the canopy, looking for fruit, insects or eggs to eat. It cannot leap from tree to tree as monkeys can.

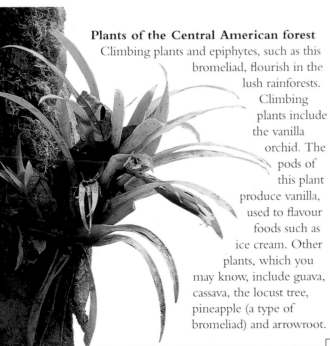

Plants of the Central American forest

Climbing plants and epiphytes, such as this bromeliad, flourish in the lush rainforests. Climbing plants include the vanilla orchid. The pods of this plant produce vanilla, used to flavour foods such as ice cream. Other plants, which you may know, include guava, cassava, the locust tree, pineapple (a type of bromeliad) and arrowroot.

Ocelot

The ocelot is one of the few large mammals that live in Central American forests. The spots and stripes on every ocelot's coat are different, making it as individual as a fingerprint. But many of these beautiful creatures have been killed for their fur, and they are now quite rare.

THE AMAZON

THE Amazon jungle in South America is the world's largest tropical rainforest. The forest covers the basin of the Amazon, one of the world's longest rivers. As it flows towards the sea, thousands of smaller rivers and streams join this great river to swell the waters. In most places the Amazon is only a few kilometres across, but it widens as it gets nearer the Atlantic Ocean, until the banks are over 60 km apart and the river looks like a sea. The Amazon is home to the greatest variety of plants and animals on Earth. A fifth of all the world's plants and birds are found there and about one tenth of all mammal species. Many more species are waiting to be discovered and identified by scientists. Forest birds include the colourful ibis and the toucan with its enormous beak. The many kinds of mammals that live in the forest include the predatory jaguar, the scaly armadillo and the slow-moving sloth.

Amerindians
Children bathe in the river while their mothers wash clothes in the water. Many different groups of Amerindian people live in the forest. They are used to the changing levels of the river and net fish and farm their crops as the water rises and falls at different times of the year.

Scarlet ibis
The scarlet ibis lives in the swampy areas of rainforest. It has long stilt-like legs on which it wades through the mud, probing with its beak for frogs and fishes. For years, it has been hunted for its brilliant plumage.

Ginger flowers
This long-stemmed plant grows throughout lowland areas of the Amazon rainforest. One species of ginger flower produces edible, knobbly roots. These are used fresh or dried, pickled or preserved to flavour food. The shoots, leaves and flowers are also eaten raw or cooked.

Hoatzin

The hoatzin nests in the mangrove forests of the Amazon. The size of a chicken, the hoatzin is an ungainly bird. It is a poor flier and can only manage short flights along the river. Young birds have two tiny claws on the front of each wing, which help them to climb trees.

Armoured armadillo

Armadillos are shy creatures. They rest by day and come out at night to root for worms and insects in the forest soil. The armadillo's body is covered by a protective layer of bony plates. When threatened, the creature rolls itself up into a tight, scaly ball.

Poison-arrow frog

The blue poison-arrow frog is one of several South American species with very poisonous skin. The poison stops hungry predators from eating the frog. It is also used by Amerindian hunters, who tip their blow-pipe darts with the poison when they go hunting.

Toco toucan

The toucan is one of the best-known jungle birds. The toco toucan shown here has one of the largest beaks of any bird. The beak is partly hollow and not as heavy as it looks. It allows the toucan to reach forest berries dangling beyond the reach of most other creatures.

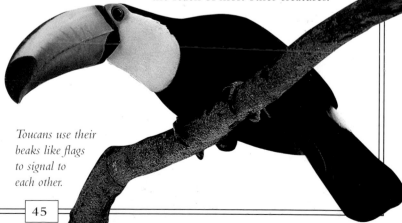

Toucans use their beaks like flags to signal to each other.

AFRICA

THE rainforests of Africa lie in a band across the west and centre of the continent, on either side of the Equator. Central Africa holds the world's second largest rainforest. To the southeast, the large island of Madagascar was also once largely forested, but much of this jungle has now been felled. Central Africa contains areas of high cloud forest, mangrove swamps and flooded forest, as well as lowland jungle. A wide variety of plants and animals are found in these different habitats. Bamboo and palm trees grow in the understorey below the forest canopy, which is topped by tall, straight-trunked hardwood trees. Many forest animals, including chameleons, okapi and spotted leopards, rely on camouflage to hide from their enemies or creep up on prey. The island of Madagascar is home to many unique plants and animals found nowhere else. The forests of West Africa once contained many magnificent mahogany trees, but most of these tropical hardwood trees have been cut down for their precious timber. In West Africa today the forest survives only in small pockets near the coast.

White fronted lemur
Thirty different species live on Madagascar. They are closely related to monkeys. Most roam the forest in small groups looking for fruit and insects.

Chimpanzee
The lowland forests of Central Africa make an ideal habitat for chimpanzees. These small apes are among the world's most intelligent creatures. They use stones as hammers and poke twigs inside the nests of termites to fish out the insects to eat. Chimpanzees feed mainly on fruit and leaves, but also eat meat. They make up organized hunting parties to catch pigs, deer or smaller monkeys.

FACTBOX

• The forests of Central Africa alone are home to more than 8,000 different species of plants.

• Madagascar contains two-thirds of the world's chameleon species. These lizards have the amazing ability to change their skin colour to match their surroundings by making different coloured clumps of cells in their skin bigger or smaller.

Ground gecko

Geckos are lizards. This one lives on the forest floor in Madagascar. Its body is camouflaged to disguise the lizard as it scuttles among the leaves.

Jungle songbird

Orioles are found in the rainforests of Africa and southern Asia. They feed on fruit and insects and are known for their beautiful song. This black-headed oriole is keeping a sharp look-out for predators.

Okapi

These large grazing animals are related to giraffes. They live deep in lowland rainforests, feeding on leaves which they tear off jungle plants with their long tongues. The okapi has stripes on its legs and hide. This enables the animal's outline to blend in with the dappled vegetation, protecting it from predators.

Hornbill

A red-billed hornbill preens its feathers to keep them clean and in good condition. Many different kinds of hornbill live in lowland forests. They make their nests in tree trunks and lay their eggs inside. The male bird walls up the nest hole with mud, to protect the female and the young inside from predators. He leaves a tiny hole to feed his family.

47

SOUTHERN ASIA

THE rainforests of Asia stretch from India and Myanmar (Burma) in the west to Malaysia and the islands of Java and Borneo in the east. The area includes Sundarbans in Bangladesh – the largest area of mangrove forest in the world. Most of mainland Asia has a sub-tropical climate with torrential monsoon rains followed by a drier period. In Southeast Asia it is hot and humid all year round. Rainforest trees include rattan palms, rubber trees and giant tropical hardwoods, such as teak, ebony and rosewood. Other jungle plants include bamboo, ginger, orchids and rafflesia – the world's largest flower. Indian jungles are home to peacocks and deadly cobras. Elephants, tigers and buffalo live in forest clearings. Large areas of Asian rainforest have been chopped down for fuel, or burned down to make room for crops. Southeast Asian animals include gibbons, orang-utans and the rare Sumatran rhino.

Peacock's display
Peacocks have the most spectacular tail feathers of any bird. When courting a female, the male spreads his tail and quivers his fan of feathery eyes. Asian forests are also home to golden pheasants and red jungle fowl – the ancestor of the domestic chicken.

Giant rafflesia
Rafflesia, the world's largest flower, blooms on the forest floor in Sumatra. The flowers can measure up to 1 m across and give off a strong smell like rotting meat. Rafflesia is a parasite, living on the roots of some jungle vines. The flower's scent attracts insects that pollinate the plant.

Hidden creature
Rafflesia flowers are so huge that tiny mammals like this tree shrew can shelter inside. The flowers provide a good source of insects for shrews to feed on.

Gibbon

This ape hangs from a branch in Borneo. Gibbons swing from hand to hand to move through the treetops at great speed.

Flying lizard

This special lizard is diving through the air in Sumatra. The flying lizard has extra-long rib bones, which are connected by a flap of skin. This flap can be spread like a frilly skirt, allowing the lizard to glide from tree to tree. Asian rainforests are home to a number of flying animals, including the colugo, which has large flaps of skin along its body.

Asian elephant

The elephants of Asia live deep in the forest, unlike the elephants of Africa, which keep to open grasslands. They are smaller than their African relatives, with smaller ears, an arched back and a domed forehead. Females and their young live in herds led by the oldest female, known as the matriarch. They feed almost entirely on leaves.

FACT BOX

• The island of Java in Indonesia has lost 90 per cent of its rainforest. But Indonesia as a whole still holds ten per cent of the world's tropical rainforests.

• Flying animals of Asian rainforests include frogs, squirrels and snakes. These creatures do not really fly, but rather glide through the air.

AUSTRALASIA

Australian rainforest
Undergrowth in Australia's tropical forests is dense and lush. The forests lie in the path of wet winds blowing in from the Pacific.

Millions of years ago, Australia, New Zealand and the island of New Guinea formed part of a great forested southern continent, isolated from the rest of the world. Today these countries contain many similar species of animal that occur nowhere else. In Australia, tropical rainforest survives only in a thin strip along the northeastern coast. Marsupials populate much of this area. Female marsupials have a furry pouch in which to raise their young. Rainforest marsupials include tree kangaroos and sugar gliders. North of Australia, the large island of New Guinea is still mostly forested. Its wildlife is a mix of species from Australia and Southeast Asia. Bird life includes the cassowary, bower bird and birds of paradise. Mammals include the extraordinary, egg-laying echidna.

Cassowary
This ground-dwelling bird lives in the forests of New Guinea. Like the ostrich, it is a giant bird that cannot fly. The large bony crest on its head acts like a helmet as it crashes its way through the forest.

Sugar glider
The treetops of Australian rainforests are home to a small, mouse-like marsupial called a sugar glider. It has two long, furry flaps of skin between its front and back legs. The animal stretches out these furry flaps to glide from tree to tree. It feeds on insects, fruit and sugary foods such as nectar from flowers and tree sap.

Echidna

The echidna, or spiny anteater, is one of only a few mammals that lay eggs. After ten days, the eggs hatch out into tiny babies, which feed on their mother's milk. The echidna's body has a protective covering of prickly spines, like a hedgehog. It feeds on insects, mainly ants and termites, which it licks up with its long sticky tongue.

Bower bird

The female bird above has been attracted to a display site, or bower, that the male bower bird has made from grass and twigs. To court a female, the male will decorate the bower with berries, feathers and other bright objects. Unfortunately, bright objects such as blue bottle caps, may prove to be harmful to bower birds. Different species of bower bird build bowers of different shapes. Bower birds live in the forests of New Guinea and Australia.

Tree kangaroo

Like all kangaroos, tree kangaroos are marsupials. A number of different species live in Australia and New Guinea. Some can hop on the ground like the kangaroos of the outback. Others spend their whole lives in the trees and cannot hop. The long tail of this tree kangaroo helps it balance as it clambers among the branches. It is remarkably agile, despite not having feet adapted for climbing.

TEMPERATE RAINFORESTS

THE world's temperate rainforests are found in the cooler regions north and south of the tropics. The largest temperate forests occur on the northwest coast of North America, in Chile on the southern tip of South America and on South Island in New Zealand. Temperate rainforests once covered twice as much land as they take up today, but they often occur in places where the land is needed to grow crops, or build roads and towns. The trees that grow in temperate rainforests are prized by logging companies and a great many have been felled for timber. In many regions, only small patches of temperate rainforests survive today, on steep or rocky hillsides where the land is of little use for farming. The islands of Japan, for example, were also once covered by cool rainforest. Now only a tiny part of the forest survives, on the island of Yakushima. Temperate rainforests are home to a wide variety of animals, but fewer species are found there than in tropical rainforests.

Spotted owl
These owls live in the cool, wet forests of North America. They rest in trees during the day, hunting at night for small rodents such as flying squirrels.

Kiwi
New Zealand is the only place in the world where these strange, flightless birds are found. They live in burrows. At night, they scurry about the forest floor, sniffing out insects and worms to eat.

Kauri pines
These trees are found in cool forests on New Zealand's North Island. They can grow up to 55 m tall and live for 2,000 years. This kauri pine, named Tane Mahuta, or Lord of the Forest, is the largest in New Zealand.

Olympic National Park, Washington state

Shrubs, ferns, mosses and a large variety of trees grow in this cool rainforest. The northwest coast of North America has a high rainfall because it is swept by wet winds blowing in from the Pacific.

Mule deer

These deer roam the temperate forests of North America from Alaska to northern Mexico. These shy creatures are hard to spot among the forest trees. They are called mule deer because of their long, mule-like ears.

Quoll

This tiger cat lives in the mountainous rainforests of Tasmania and eastern Australia. It is an aggressive marsupial with a spotted coat. It survives by hunting birds, insects and mammals.

Tasmanian devil

This ferocious animal can be found only on the island of Tasmania off southern Australia. The western part of Tasmania is covered with temperate rainforest. The Tasmanian devil lives among eucalyptus woods. It is the largest surviving, meat-eating marsupial. Up to 1 m long, it feeds mainly on carrion (dead animals).

FOREST SKILLS

THE animals of rainforests and other woodland areas are cautious and quick-witted. Their keen eyesight, sharp hearing and good sense of smell allow them to sense you long before you know that they are there. The only way to get close to forest animals is to be patient and keep very quiet and still.

MATERIALS

You will need: warm hat, scarf, gloves, binoculars.

When going out to look for forest wildlife, wear dull-coloured clothing that blends in with the woods. Wear a warm, waterproof coat, so you do not get cold or damp. When approaching animals, move slowly and quietly. Keep behind the cover of trees or bushes, so the animals do not notice you. Sometimes the signs wild animals leave are easier to spot than the animals themselves. Animal homes, such as nests and burrows, are easy to find. Hair, half-eaten food and droppings all show that animals have passed this way.

In Madagascar, experts use radio transmitters to track lemurs and other animals.

Stalking animals

1 When stalking animals in the wild, move slowly and put your feet down carefully. Step softly on fallen leaves, which will rustle to give you away. Try to avoid dry twigs that will crack.

2 Try to keep behind the cover of trees or shrubs that will hide you from wild animals. If you spot an animal, drop down on all fours and creep forward slowly.

3 If it is windy, try to approach animals downwind – with the wind blowing in your face. Otherwise your scent will give you away. To find out which way the wind is blowing, wet your finger and hold it up to feel the breeze.

Finding animal signs

1 A hole in a forest tree shows that a bird has nested there. This hole was drilled out by a woodpecker. Your field guide will have details of the birds that nest in this way.

2 Animals that burrow into the earth leave clear signs of their presence. These holes were made by rabbits. Fresh earth and droppings show that the burrow is in use.

3 Gnawed bark, half-eaten fruit or broken twigs are all signs of animals feeding. The bark of this tree was gnawed by deer when food was scarce in winter.

MATERIALS

You will need: gloves, notebook, pencil, magnifying glass, binoculars, field guide.

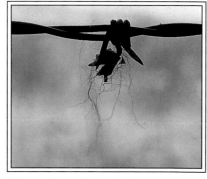

4 Some mammals sharpen their claws on tree trunks, leaving scratch marks. These scratches were made by a badger and show that this part of the forest is occupied.

5 Droppings show where animals have fed. These were left by a fox. Some animals leave piles of dung to mark their territory – the area where they hunt for food.

6 Look out for animal fur caught in barbed wire or on the bottom of wooden fences. Notice the colour and texture of the hair. This hair belonged to a badger.

PEOPLES OF THE RAINFOREST

There are about a thousand different tribes, or groups, of peoples living in rainforests around the world. These peoples have lived in the forest for hundreds or even thousands of years, and take what they need from the forest without harming it. Peoples, such as the Yanomami of the Amazon basin and the Huli of New Guinea, gather fruit and vegetables from the forest and hunt animals for meat. Their tools and weapons are traditionally made from materials such as wood. Plants collected from the forest are used as medicines. Some groups grow gardens of crops around their villages. They farm in ways that do not destroy the forest. The well-being of many rainforest peoples is threatened by the ever-shrinking forest and by disease, logging, farming and mining. In some rainforest countries, governments have encouraged people from the cities to settle in the forest. The new settlers often farm in ways that harm the forest and bring diseases such as chickenpox and mumps, which can kill the local people.

Growing crops
Native peoples clear patches of forest to grow crops. Then they move on, allowing the forest to grow back.

Forest hunters
This man from the Amazon rainforest has killed an armadillo. Amerindians are skilful hunters. They use traps, bows and arrows and blowpipes that fire darts tipped with poison. Nowadays guns are also used, making the hunters even more efficient.

The Pygmies
This Pygmy woman is cooking food outside her hut, with her baby cradled on her back. Mbuti and Baka Pygmies live in the rainforests of Central Africa. Traditionally they live by hunting and gathering food.

Huli warrior

The Huli are one of many tribes that live in the remote highland rainforests of Papua New Guinea. They live by hunting, gathering plants and growing crops. Men and women live separately, in large group houses. The men decorate their bodies with coloured clay and wear elaborate headdresses for ceremonies.

Old and new

Like many rainforest peoples of Southeast Asia, the Lemenak still build houses made of traditional local materials, such as wood and bamboo. This grandmother is weaving a basket from leaves, while looking after her grandaughter in a hammock made of more modern materials.

The Yanomami

One of the largest groups of Amerindian people in South America is the Yanomami. Their village life is centred round the yano, or communal house. The yano is a large, circular building constructed of vine and leaf thatch, which has a living space in the middle. This picture shows Yanomami men eating a meal.

FACT BOX

• The Amerindians of South America once used the roots of jungle vines to make curare, a deadly poison for their arrows. Now scientists use curare to make a drug to relax muscles.

• 140 different peoples live in the Brazilian rainforest.

RAINFOREST SHELTER

People who live in rainforests build their homes from materials found in the forest. Houses provide protection from heavy rain and fierce jungle animals. In South America, the Yanomami's large, round huts are made with trees bent into a dome shape, lashed with vines and thatched with palm leaves. The roofed area is used for sleeping – the Yanomami sleep in hammocks made of woven grasses, slung from the rafters. Scientists working in rainforests sometimes build temporary shelters with branches and waterproof material. They also sleep in hammocks. You can build a simple shelter by following these instructions. This project will require careful thought and the help of an adult. When looking for branches to make your shelter with, take an adult with you. Collect the branches from your garden or a public area. Do not cut branches from trees, always gather them from the ground - where they have fallen naturally.

Longhouses

In Peru, houses are built on stilts to protect against flooding. Large communal huts, called longhouses, may contain as many as 100 families. The hut is reached by a ladder pulled up at night.

Build a shelter

1 Lash the ends of two sturdy branches together with strong rope. Stand the branches upright to make an A-frame. You could tie the A-frame to a tree for extra support.

2 Lash two more branches together. Stand them upright about 2 m from the first A-frame. Place a lighter branch on top to make a ridge pole and lash in place.

3 Attach two guy-ropes to each of the A-frames and peg the guy-ropes securely into the ground. Now throw a tarpaulin over the ridge pole to form the roof.

4 Attach guy-ropes or strings to eyeholes in the corners of the tarpaulin and peg them securely into ground. Stretch the tarpaulin tight to make the roof.

5 Thread string through the eyeholes on opposite sides of the ground sheet to make the sheet into a sort of tube. Push two poles inside the sheet, one on each side.

6 Pull the two poles apart to make a stretcher shape that will fit inside the shelter. This will form the hammock so that you will be able to rest off the ground.

MATERIALS

You will need: five sturdy branches, rope or thick string, tarpaulin, scissors, string or guy-ropes, eight pegs, ground sheet, two poles, a friend or adult to help.

Make sure your hammock is secure and will not slip down the poles before you lie on it. Now you can take a well-earned rest!

7 Wedge the stretcher inside your shelter, so that the poles rest on the outside of the upright A-frames.

RAINFOREST PRODUCE

THE world's tropical rainforests seem remote, but their produce is all around us and part of our everyday lives. Without rainforests, there would be no rubber, sugar or chocolate. Next time you visit a supermarket, look at the labels to see how many of your favourite foods come from these forests. Bananas, lemons, pineapples and avocados all come from tropical jungles. So do many kinds of nuts, including peanuts, cashews and brazils. Coffee beans and kola nuts are used to make coffee and cola drinks. Other rainforest plants produce spices such as ginger, nutmeg, cinnamon and pepper to flavour our food. All these products come from plants that first grew wild in rainforests. Now many of them are grown for the world market in large plantations. Rainforest produce also includes hardwoods, such as ebony, mahogany and rosewood, used for building and making furniture. When trees are cut down for timber or forests cleared for plantations, however, wild plants and animals suffer.

Chewing gum

The sapodilla, or chicle tree, produces a milky sap that thickens when heated. The Aztecs chewed gum from the chicle tree, our gum also comes from this rainforest tree.

Growing sugar

Most sugar is made from sugar cane, a giant tropical grass. This popular food plant is now grown in plantations all over the world. In Jamaica, pictured here, and many other areas, native plants and animals have been disturbed as forest land is cleared to make plantations.

Oil palms

Here, young oil palms are being watered in Costa Rica. Oil from the fruit of mature palms is made into cooking oil and used in soap, shampoo and cosmetics. Oil palms originally grew in West Africa, but they are now found in tropical regions all over the world.

Bamboo

A worker harvests bamboo, cutting through the thick stems with a sharp knife called a machete. Bamboo is an amazing rainforest plant. It is actually a giant, fast-growing grass, not a tree. The tough stems of bamboo are used for building houses and for scaffolding poles. Bamboo canes are also used for weaving baskets, building furniture and making musical instruments.

Rubber is dyed before it is moulded into shape.

Healing plants

Rainforests have traditionally been a great source of herbs and medicines for peoples of the rainforests. Scientists have only discovered the medicinal powers of a small proportion of these plants. Quinine from the cinchona tree (*above*) is used to treat malaria and make tonic water (*above right*). The rosy periwinkle from Madagascar is used to treat a form of cancer called leukaemia.

Rubber harvest

Natural rubber is made from a sticky sap, called latex, which oozes from the bark of rainforest trees. To harvest the sap, grooves are cut in the bark. The latex runs down into a little cup hung on the trunk. Rubber is used to make a very wide range of products, from hot water bottles and car tyres to elastic bands, golf balls and tennis balls.

SAVING THE RAINFORESTS

THE world's rainforests are currently disappearing at a rate of 2,400 hectares every hour. When forests are cut down, the plants and animals that live in that habitat are put at risk. Scientists believe that much wildlife in the rainforests has not yet been discovered. They fear some species will die out before they have even been identified. So what is being done to stop the destruction? Recently people have realized that rainforests are a vital resource for the whole world. We rely on them for many different products, including precious medicines. Rainforests affect the weather for hundreds of kilometres around, bringing rain and keeping the air well-oxygenated. Developed countries and rainforest nations now meet at international conferences to plan ways to conserve, or save, the forests. There are many different things that can be done. Forests can be managed more effectively, with controlled logging and the planting of new trees. National parks and reserves can also be set up to protect the wildlife.

Tigers
Asian tigers need a large area in which to hunt. As the forests where they live are cut down, so their numbers fall.

Sumatran rhinoceros
This Sumatran rhino is wallowing in a cooling mud bath. Only a few hundred of these magnificent animals survive in the wild. Hunting, and the destruction of its habitat, mean that soon they may die out altogether. Those surviving can be found in Southeast Asia, apart from a few individuals left in zoos.

Mountain gorilla
Gorillas found in the upland rainforests of eastern Africa are also under threat. They face a shrinking habitat and death by poachers. Reserves have now been set up to try and save them.

Planting trees

A worker tends seedlings at a tree nursery in Ghana. These trees will be planted to replace those that have been cut down for timber. Hardwood trees, however, grow very slowly, and it will be many years before these young trees are forest giants. Another way to save rainforest trees is to use softwood timber to make furniture. Softwood trees grow much more quickly, so they are easier to replace.

Golden lion tamarin

This rare monkey is found only in coastal rainforests in South America. Forty years ago they came close to extinction (dying out). People had killed the monkeys, mistakenly believing they spread disease. Then survivors were bred in captivity in the United States and Europe. Now numbers of golden lion tamarins have been released back into the wild.

Breeding orang-utans

Orang-utans (*on the left of this picture*) are being fed in a breeding centre in Borneo. Orang-utans are large forest apes from Borneo and Sumatra. Their name means Man of the Forest. The survival of these large apes has been threatened by deforestation, but they are now being bred in captivity. Tourists come to see the animals being reared and bring much-needed money to the area.

People power

An Amerindian protests at an international conference about the destruction of the Amazon rainforest. Recently, rainforest people have begun to demand a say in what happens to the forests in which they live. They fight plans to build new mines, roads or dams in their area if they feel the new development will harm their way of life.

INDEX

PICTURE CREDITS
b=bottom, t=top, c=centre, l=left, r=right
Bruce Coleman Limited: 4r, 6tr, 6bl, 6br, 7t, 7bl, 8b, 9br, 10t, 12t, 12bl, 12br, 13t, 13br, 16br, 17bl, 17br, 18t, 21br, 24b, 25tr, 26br, 29t, 30tr, 32t, 33b, 33t, 36t, 37c, 37b, 38t, 39tr, 39br, 40t, 42bc, 42t, 43t, 43bl, 43br, 45bl, 45br, 47tl, 47bl, 47br, 48bl, 48br, 49tr, 49b, 50bl, 51t, 51br, 52bl, 52br, 53tr, 53cr, 55tr, 60bl and 62t.
Ecoscene: 21tl. Frank Lane Picture Agency: 9tr, 16t, 17t, 20t, 21bl, 25bl, 25br, 27tl, 28t, 28br, 29c, 34bl, 34bc, 34br, 44bl, 45tl, 46b, 48t, 50t, 50br, 53tl, 53b,55tl, 55tc, 55bl, 55bc, 55br, 56br, 62bl and 63tr.
Garden and Wildlife Matters Photo Library: 29b. Holt Studios International: 28bl, 44br, 58t, 61c and 63tl. Hutchison Library: 56t and 56bl. Natural History Photographic Agency: 25tl, 36bl, 36br, 37t, 44t, 45tr and 54t. Natural Science Photos: 33c. Papilio Photographic Agency: 7br, 8t, 9tl, 13bl, 16bl, 39tl, 39bl, 42c, 46t, 49tl, 51bl, 57tr, 60br, 61tr, 61br,62br and 63bl. Planet Earth Pictures: 24t, 32bl, 34t and 47tr. Still Pictures: 63br. Trip/ J Wakelin: 57tl. Zefa Pictures: 52t and 57b.